TRUST, TRUTH, AND RIDICULOUS GOOFS

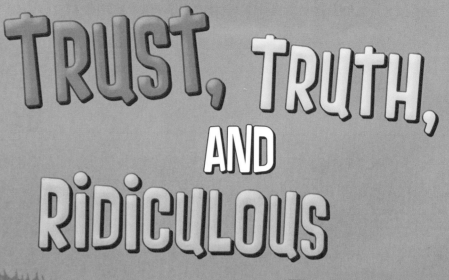

Reading and Writing
Friendship Poems

compiled and annotated by Jill Kalz

PICTURE WINDOW BOOKS
a capstone imprint

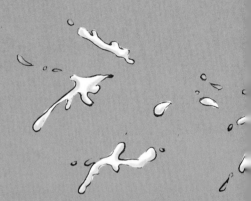

Special thanks to our adviser for his expertise:

Terry Flaherty, PhD, Professor of English
Minnesota State University, Mankato

Editor: Jill Kalz
Designer: Lori Bye
Art Director: Nathan Gassman
Production Specialist: Kathy McColley

Illustration Credits
Cristian Bernardini, cover, 4, 5, 6, 15, 16-17, 20-21, 28, 29, 32; Dustin Burkes-Larrañaga, 1, 8, 18, 23; Sandra D'Antonio, 7, 24, 31;
Matt Loveridge, back cover, 2-3, 10-11, 19, 22, 26-27; Simon Smith, 14; Shutterstock: KennyK, 9; Tou Yia Xiong, 12, 13, 25

Picture Window Books are published by Capstone,
1710 Roe Crest Drive, North Mankato, Minnesota 56003
www.capstonepub.com

Library of Congress Cataloging-in-Publication Data
Cataloging-in-publication information is on file with the Library of Congress.
ISBN 978-1-4795-2199-9 (library binding)
ISBN 978-1-4795-2950-6 (paperback)
ISBN 978-1-4795-3333-6 (eBook PDF)

Printed in the United States of America in Brainerd, Minnesota.
092013   007770BANGS14

TABLE OF CONTENTS

DISCOVER THE POET IN YOU

Maybe you have one best friend. Or 10! Maybe your best friend is your brother. Maybe it's your pet gerbil! No matter who or what your best friend is, friendships are amazing. And no two friendships are exactly the same. You can celebrate your friends by writing poems about them. Share how they cheer you up when you're down. Write about the time lemonade shot out of their noses when they laughed.

WHY WRITE POETRY?

When you write poetry, you're an explorer. You discover new words, new combinations of words, and new meanings. You use old words in fresh ways. Poetry opens your ears. Sentences can play like music. Poetry opens your eyes. It's as if you're seeing the world around you—your ordinary, everyday world—for the very first time. Poetry can be a new language that allows you to share your ideas and experiences.

WHAT TOOLS DOES A POET USE?

Whether you're building a house, a car, or a video game, you need tools to get the job done. Poets use tools to build their poems too. Their tools include parts of speech (such as nouns, verbs, and adjectives), ways of writing (like different forms or types of poetry), and the cool sounds that letters and words make when they're combined (like rhymes and repeated letters). Knowing what the tools are and how to use them is what this book is all about.

HOW DO I READ THIS BOOK?

Start by reading the poems. All of them are about friendship. After you read each one, take a look at the Info Box on the bottom of the page. There you'll find definitions of poetic forms and tools. You may also find helpful tips, questions to consider, or writing prompts. Near the back of the book, you'll have the chance to review what you've learned and practice writing your own poems. Before you know it, you'll be a poet!

Pink Lemonade

I once had a good friend named Jade
Who loved to drink pink lemonade.
'Til I tickled her toes,
And it shot out her nose—
What a spectacular geyser she made!

—Christopher L. Harbo

SOUNDS LIKE ...

When words end in the same sound, they **rhyme**. In the poem above, "Jade," "lemonade," and "made" rhyme. So do "toes" and "nose." Rhyming words can add interest and structure to a poem. Try making a list of words that rhyme with "pink."

The Squirrel

Hopping on our porch
and then nibbling one brown nut,
squirrel looks up and winks.

—Connie Colwell Miller

A **haiku** is a Japanese form of poetry. It has three lines and follows a 5-7-5 pattern of **syllables**. Lines 1 and 3 have five syllables. Line 2 has seven. The poem above is short, but it tells us a lot. For starters, we learn that a squirrel is visiting. What else do we learn?

Fishing with My Uncle

Teddy's my mother's oldest brother.
He likes to tell the oddest fish stories,
Especially about the ones that got away.

Once, he said, *I nearly caught*
Nine walleyes *all at the same time,*
Each fish nipping the tail of the next.

They were fighting over my lucky spinner,
He said. *A lure made of wire,*
A Barq's bottle cap and a sparkly shoelace.
The best stories, of course, include me.

Golly! he'd start. *You really had a big un*
On the hook. We didn't have a nibble all day,
Though that wouldn't stop Uncle Teddy.

Almost pulled my niece right out of the boat.
Whale shark, *that's what it must have been.*
And I would just sit and grin and giggle,
You know, because this is what uncles do.

—Blake Hoena

HIDDEN MESSAGES

An **acrostic** is a poem that can be read in two directions. When the first letter of each line is put together, it spells another word or phrase. Sometimes that hidden message is the poem's main idea or title. What's the hidden message in the poem above?

Ball and Glove

Ball likes
to fly, and Glove
to catch. Without friendship,
poor Ball feels lost, and Glove empty
inside.

—Blake Hoena

TAKE FIVE

A **cinquain** (sin-CANE) is a five-line poem. "Cinq" means "five" in French. The poem follows a 2-4-6-8-2 pattern of syllables.

Count the syllables in the poem above with your fingers. Feel the pattern? Count with your fingers when you write too. It'll help!

Little Louie's Friend

There once was a small dog,
a pug to be exact.
His name was Little Louie,
and his fur was lush and black.

Little Louie loved his life.
He liked to romp and play.
He often nosed a ball around,
pushing back and forth all day.

FEEL THE BEAT

Rhythm is the "drum" in poetry. It can be created by **beats** or syllables. You can measure rhythm in **meter**—just count the beats or stressed syllables in each line. Read aloud, and tap the beats with your finger: "There ONCE was A small DOG ..."

But sometimes Louie felt alone,
rolling balls around the yard.
He thought a partner in this life
might make the game less hard.

Then one day out in the yard,
a brand new pup came round.
It was a pug, just like Lou,
but his fur was soft and brown.

Little Louie rolled the ball
to his brand new puggish friend.
And from that day, the two pug dogs
were friends until the end.

—Connie Colwell Miller

A Boy and His Dog

A boy and his dog racing down the street
Excited to go wherever they go
She chases a squirrel and sniffs a tree

He laughs as he's pulled along by her leash
Oh what fun they will have they never know
A boy and his dog racing down the street

They splash through puddles on a muddy beach
They romp around the yard covered in snow
She chases a squirrel and sniffs a tree

He turns away as she squats down to pee
They run down the block and they run back home
A boy and his dog racing down the street

Who owns who the eternal mystery
For these best friends never go it alone
She chases a squirrel and sniffs a tree

He leads her home when it's time for a treat
A cookie for him and for her a bone
Then they are off and racing down the street
They will chase squirrels even in their sleep

—Blake Hoena

OVER AND OVER

When poets use **repetition**, they repeat certain words, phrases, or sounds. Repetition can help create patterns. It can also help make a point. The poem above repeats two phrases. Why do you think the poet changes them slightly in the final two lines?

Jumping Bikes

Hey! Hey! Look at me!
I'm stuck in a tree!
But how did I reach this position?

My best friend, Lee Spikes,
Built a ramp for our bikes
That put me in this sad condition.

Who knew that his jump
Would give such a bump
As to launch me to this height?

But I pedaled too hard,
I cleared the whole yard,
And now I must make quite a sight.

With arms and legs tangled,
And my bike clearly mangled,
Lee ran off to search for my dad.

But I think I may be
Better off in this tree,
'Cause, boy, he is going to be mad.

—Christopher L. Harbo

STORYTELLING

Narrative poems tell stories. They may be long or short, rhyming or not. The stories may be simple or complex. They may include action and **dialogue**. What details does this poet use to build excitement and keep you interested in the poem's story?

The Very Best Friend

A little boy, ten years old,
has the best friend in the world.
One day, at lunch, they shrink down small
and dive into their noodles. Up to their ears
in macaroni, they eat and eat and eat.
Soon there's just one noodle left, so the boy
and his friend hop on it. They ride up the slippery
bowl and, in a wink, they're soaring. They land,
splash! in chocolate milk, then breaststroke through
with mouths wide open, guzzling, guzzling, gone!
Then, resting at the bottom of the glass,
inside a milky bubble, the boy and his friend
each let out a huge and happy belch.
This little boy, that special day, so happy with his friend.
Who is his friend? His wonderful imagination.

—Connie Colwell Miller

BE FREE

A **free verse** poem doesn't follow a fixed rhythm or meter. Repeating sounds or words may help hold the poem together. Here the words "ten / best / friend," "land / splash," "eat and eat and eat," and "guzzling, guzzling, gone" create interest.

Everyone Knows What It's Like to Be Shy

So shy, she slides by
like a snail in a spiral shell,
                    trying to hide.

She stands against the white wall,
hoping to fade fast
                    as a ghost.

Kids in her class, curious and kind,
see her shyness and think up a plan.

Some switch into snails
and slowly slide by her side
                    to say hello.

Others wish themselves invisible.
Like good ghosts they glide over
                    and whisper welcoming words.

Then all snails and ghosts turn back into kids,
and the shy girl is surrounded by friends.

—Jennifer Fandel

SIDE-BY-SIDE SOUNDS

Alliteration is a tool that creates interest in a poem. It repeats leading consonant sounds that are the same. In the poem above, "white wall" and "fade fast" are examples of alliteration. Find all the examples for the letter "s." How about "k"?

15

Higher and Higher

I push you on the swing
　　your feet lift off the ground

Then you push me and I
　　rise weightless into the air

I push you and you shout
　　higher higher I wanna go higher
　　rising above the swing's top bar

Then you push me so high
　　I could reach out and touch the leaves
　　laughing in the wind if I dared

I push you and watch you rise
　　above the trees and the town's
　　water tower I can see my house
　　　from up here you howl

16

You push me so high into the sky
  my toes poke a cloud, stirring it
    changing it from a winged dragon
      to a turtle riding a motorcycle

I push you higher and higher
  until your feet scrape the bottom
    of an airplane headed for Boise, Idaho,
      where your grandma Esther lives

Then you push me and gravity
  loosens its hold as I come face to face
    with the silvery man on the moon wish I
      had a friend to push me on a swing he says.

I push with all my might
  and when the swing finally comes
    back down to Earth its seat is empty
      except for a note saying *thank you*
        for the friend—the man on the moon

—Blake Hoena

A **stanza** is a group of lines that is usually separated by a blank line, called a **stanza break**. Stanzas often contain complete thoughts or images. In this poem, each stanza is a push of the swing—the friends taking turns. The breaks create pauses.

17

What Happened to My Friend the Space Alien?

friend
green, bug-eyed
buzzing, vaporizing, exploring
spaceship, galaxy, black hole, gravity
pulling, yanking, vacuuming
long, endless
wormhole

—Blake Hoena

LIKE A DIAMOND

The diamond-shaped **diamante** uses a parts-of-speech pattern. The seven-line poem starts with a noun. Two adjectives and three verbs follow. Next come four nouns, three verbs, and two adjectives. The final noun is often the opposite of the first.

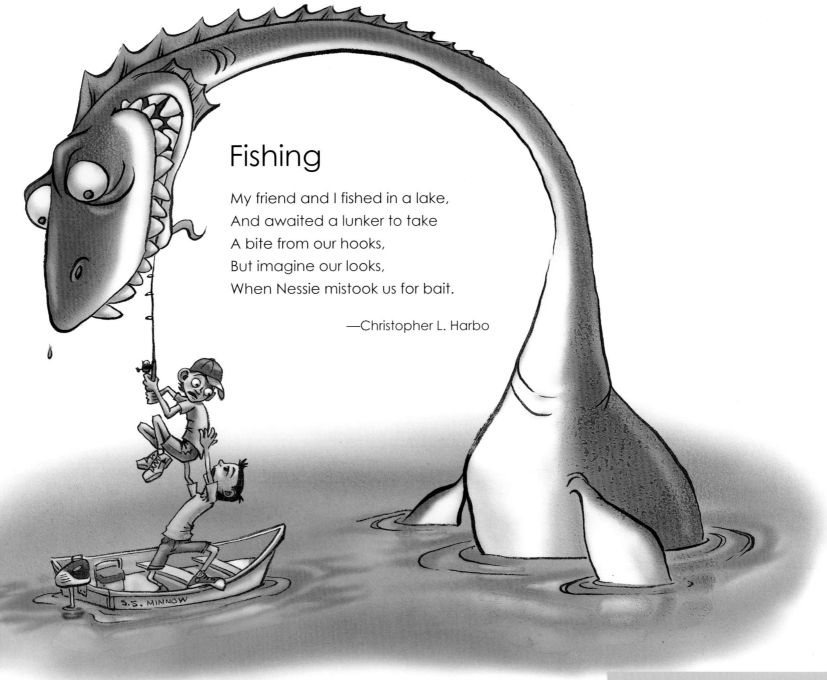

Fishing

My friend and I fished in a lake,
And awaited a lunker to take
A bite from our hooks,
But imagine our looks,
When Nessie mistook us for bait.

—Christopher L. Harbo

A **limerick** is a silly five-line poem. The first, second, and last lines rhyme ("lake / take / bait"). The third and fourth lines are shorter and rhyme with each other ("hooks / looks"). Try writing a limerick about a day with your own good friend.

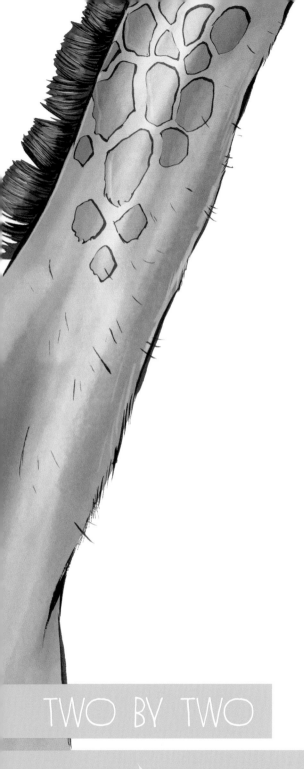

Yellow-Billed Oxpecker

Said the oxpecker to the giraffe

Does that fly make you itchy
Does that tick make you twitchy

Then be my friend, Giraffe
We'll have some good laughs

Said the giraffe to the oxpecker

When I stretch my long neck
There are spots I can't check

So I'll be your best friend
If you make this itching end

So the yellow-billed oxpecker
Pecked here and pecked there

He gobbled bug after bug
And became Giraffe's best bud

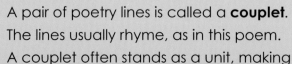

TWO BY TWO

20

A pair of poetry lines is called a **couplet**. The lines usually rhyme, as in this poem. A couplet often stands as a unit, making its own image or point. Try rewriting the final line so the bird *doesn't* get eaten. Be sure to rhyme with the word "stop."

Said the oxpecker to the zebra

  Does that fly make you itchy
  Does that tick make you twitchy

  Then be my friend, Zebra
  And I'll cure that eczema

Said the zebra to the oxpecker

  Oh my stripes are a'crawling
  I'm about to start bawling

  I just can't take a nap
  With these bugs on attack

So the yellow-billed oxpecker
Pecked here and pecked there

He plucked clean Zebra's hair
And they made a happy pair

Said the oxpecker to the crocodile

  Does that fly make you itchy
  Does that tick make you twitchy

  Be my friend, Crocodile
  And I'll clean up your smile

Said the crocodile to the oxpecker

  There's a bug between my teeth
  I wonder if you could reach

  Just a little more so don't stop
  CHOMP!

—Blake Hoena

21

Poem to Little Brothers and Little Sisters

You break my toys and make me mad.
You still take naps and won't play school.
To wash your hands, you stand on a stool.
You don't know how to read or add.

It doesn't matter if you're good or bad.
If you poke me with a stick and start a duel,
you quickly cry when you think I'm being cruel
and tell on me to Mom and Dad.

"Be friends, you two," our parents say.
Almost every day I try my best.

Our aunts and uncles show us the way.
They say Mom and Dad were also little pests.

When they were young they fought every day.
They're now best friends. Who would have guessed?

—Jennifer Fandel

SEE A PATTERN?

A poem can feel more complete when it follows a rhyming pattern. The pattern for this poem is ABBA ABBA CD CD CD. The ends of lines 1, 4, 5, and 8 rhyme ("A"). So do lines 2, 3, 6, and 7 ("B"), Which words in the poem do "C" and "D" represent?

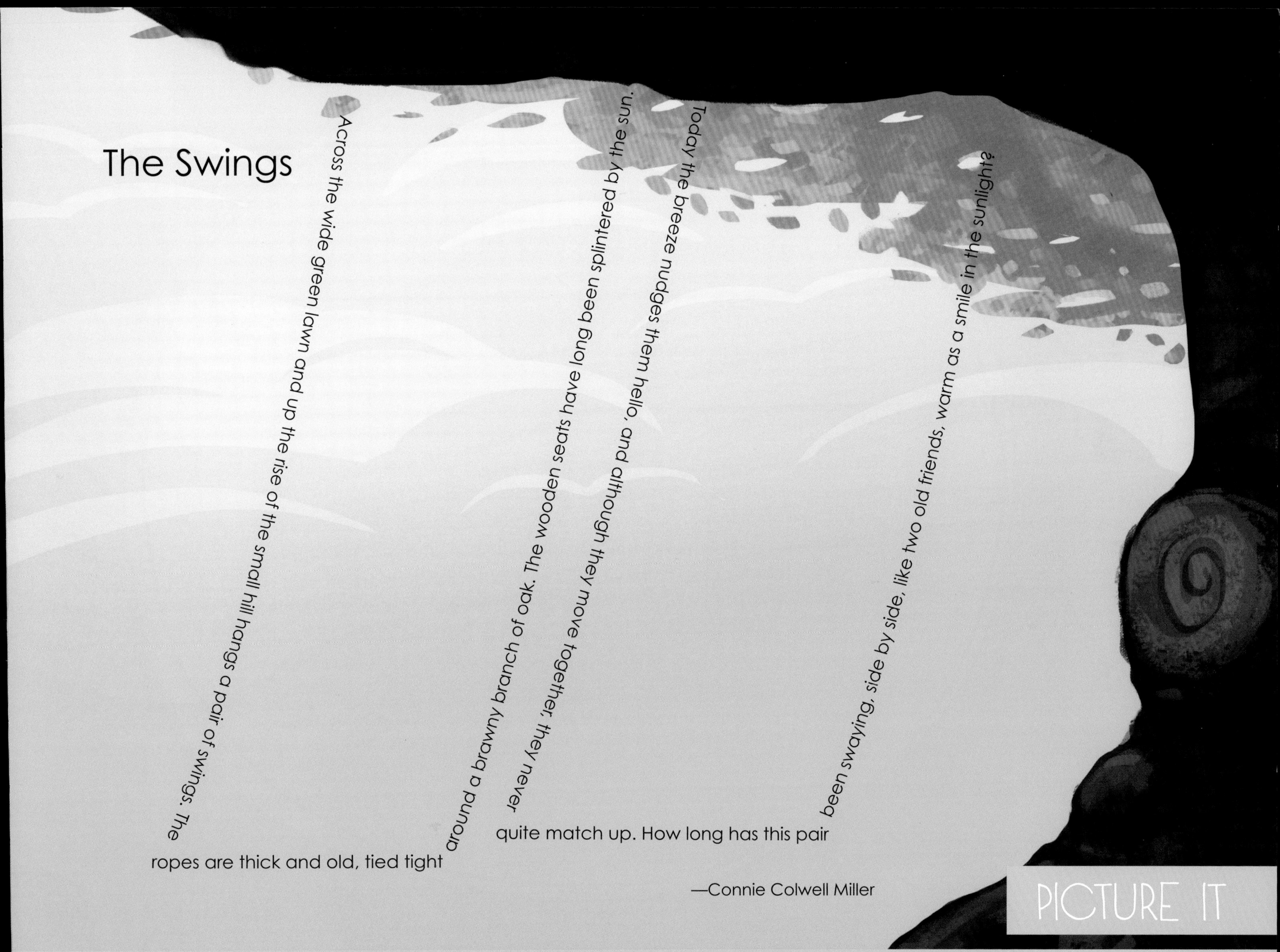

The Swings

Across the wide green lawn and up the rise of the small hill hangs a pair of swings. The ropes are thick and old, tied tight around a brawny branch of oak. The wooden seats have long been splintered by the sun. Today the breeze nudges them hello, and although they move together, they never quite match up. How long has this pair been swaying, side by side, like two old friends, warm as a smile in the sunlight?

—Connie Colwell Miller

PICTURE IT

A **concrete poem** is a picture as well as a poem. The words form the shape of the poem's subject. See how the lines in the poem above talk about swings and look like swings too? Try writing a concrete poem about two flowers or two fish.

23

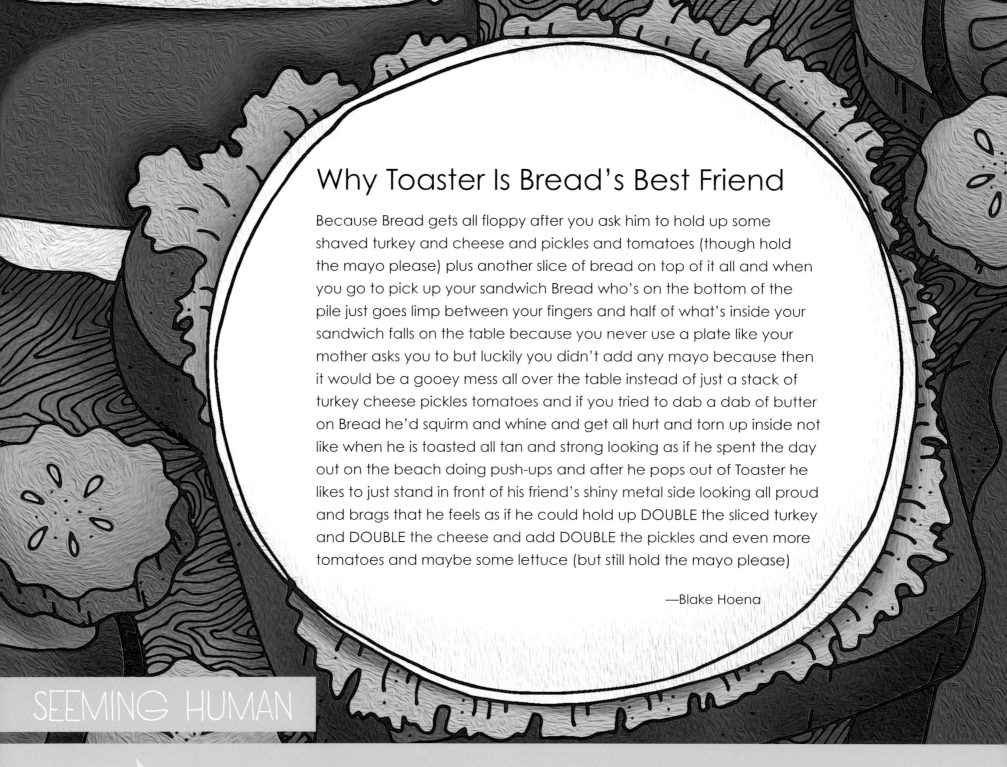

Why Toaster Is Bread's Best Friend

Because Bread gets all floppy after you ask him to hold up some shaved turkey and cheese and pickles and tomatoes (though hold the mayo please) plus another slice of bread on top of it all and when you go to pick up your sandwich Bread who's on the bottom of the pile just goes limp between your fingers and half of what's inside your sandwich falls on the table because you never use a plate like your mother asks you to but luckily you didn't add any mayo because then it would be a gooey mess all over the table instead of just a stack of turkey cheese pickles tomatoes and if you tried to dab a dab of butter on Bread he'd squirm and whine and get all hurt and torn up inside not like when he is toasted all tan and strong looking as if he spent the day out on the beach doing push-ups and after he pops out of Toaster he likes to just stand in front of his friend's shiny metal side looking all proud and brags that he feels as if he could hold up DOUBLE the sliced turkey and DOUBLE the cheese and add DOUBLE the pickles and even more tomatoes and maybe some lettuce (but still hold the mayo please)

—Blake Hoena

SEEMING HUMAN

When poets use **personification**, they make non-human things seem human. Real bread slices don't move or have feelings, but in the poem above, they do. This bread squirms and whines. And it feels sad too! See if you can personify a hammer or a turtle.

Ode to a Good Friend

The day the big dog jumped over the fence ...
The night my mom made me eat broccoli ...
The day the school bully wouldn't let me be ...
On bad days like these, only one thing makes sense.

It's not straight As or monkeys at the zoo.
It's not my favorite song or a gooey treat.
It's not even a joke from a talking parakeet,
or the clouds disappearing until the sky is bright blue.

Bad, crazy, or rainy days come to an end.
Through it all, I'm glad you're my friend.

—Jennifer Fandel

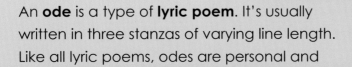

HOW I FEEL

An **ode** is a type of **lyric poem**. It's usually written in three stanzas of varying line length. Like all lyric poems, odes are personal and full of strong feelings. Here the speaker says her friend makes bad days better, even more so than what other things?

25

Of Fire and Friends: A Ballad

The fearless knight on his mighty steed
Is off on a quest to the dragon's lair.
It's riches and fame that he seeks
And the hand of a princess so fair.
He'll risk his life, or so he believes.

Now the fire-breathing dragon just hopes
To be left alone in his darkened den
And to sleep on a mountain of gold,
A birthday present that was given
To him when he turned 400 years old.

The knight pokes the dragon with his spear.
The dragon wakes with a fiery groan
And bellows, "Fearless knight, why are you here?
Why have you broken into my home?"
The knight responds while shedding a tear,

"It's for riches, for fame, and the hand
Of a princess so fair." The dragon asks,
"Then it's for love you cry, you silly man?"
"No, it's fear, for I nearly wet my pants
When you bellowed and rose up to stand.

"You're so big and have such fiery breath.
Should we fight, I'm afraid I'd get burnt."
"And I'm afraid that when my fire is spent,"
The dragon says, "that your spear will hurt
As you try to stab and poke me to death."

The fearless knight wonders what they should do.
Smoke curls out of the dragon's nostrils
As he wonders hard about it too.
"Who will die and whose blood will spill?"
The knight asks. "How can we choose?"

The dragon says, "Neither of us should die,
For I have a plan to save us both,
But it will involve a little white lie.
I will give you a handful of gold,
And you can make the princess your bride.

"You just tell everyone that I am dead,
So no more knights come pestering me."
The knight and dragon shook on it like friends.
The dragon then had a hundred-year sleep,
While the knight and princess were wed.

And all lived happily ever after. The end.

—Blake Hoena

A TALE TO TELL

A **ballad** tells a story, usually about a hero or a memorable event. It often contains action, dialogue, and a rhyming pattern.

Long ago, ballads weren't written down. They were often sung. Read this poem aloud, and try turning it into a song!

PRACTICE IT! •

Starting to understand the tools poets use? There are lots of them! The following questions will help you practice with a few tools first before you sit down to write. (Hint: Find a word you don't understand? Look in the Glossary on page 30.)

• When words end in the same sound, they rhyme, such as in the poem "Poem to Little Brothers and Little Sisters" on page 22. Find other poems in this book that have rhyming lines. Do the rhymes always appear in a pattern?

• The poem "Everyone Knows What It's Like to Be Shy" (page 15) introduced you to alliteration. Find at least three other poems that use alliteration.

• In "Higher and Higher" (page 16), the poet separates groups of lines and ideas with stanzas. Find other poems that use stanzas.

• "The Very Best Friend" (page 14) is a free verse poem—it doesn't use a pattern of rhyming words or rhythms. Find another example of free verse in this book.

• You can get a good picture of a poem because of **imagery**. Poets create imagery by using lots of details, such as colors, sounds, textures, smells, and flavors. Which poems created good pictures in your mind? What were some of the details in those poems?

• You read in "The Swings" (page 23) that the two swings sway side by side "like two old friends" because of **similes**. Similes make comparisons by saying one thing is *like* another. **Metaphors**, on the other hand, make comparisons without the use of the words "like" or "as." Find another poem that uses a simile to help describe something.

WRITE IT! •

Here's an activity that will help you discover the poet in you!

KEEP A FRIENDSHIP JOURNAL

Some of the best friendship poems come from seemingly small moments. Your friend shared her cookies with you. She said "snot" instead of "it's not." If you don't write down these moments right away, it's easy to forget them.

1) GET A PEN AND A NOTEBOOK.

Choose something small you can carry with you at all times.

2) ONCE A DAY, WRITE IN YOUR JOURNAL.

You might find it easier to remember to write if you do it at the same time every day.

3) WRITE DOWN WHATEVER GRABBED YOUR ATTENTION.

Don't forget to include all of your senses in your notes (sight, hearing, smell, taste, touch). For example:

• Laughter ... something funny your friend said or did, something funny you *both* said or did, how other people reacted, how your friend looked and sounded.

• Tears ... a sad or hurtful moment, an apology, an injury, a surprise, something scary.

• Activities ... movies, bike riding, sports, playing video games, eating pizza.

4) AT THE END OF THE WEEK, READ BACK OVER WHAT YOU'VE WRITTEN.

Choose one idea you really like—something you can see and remember clearly. Then try writing a poem about that idea. Start with a shorter poem first—a haiku, for example, rather than a ballad—until you get used to writing. Use the poems from the book as examples. "Pink Lemonade" (page 6) might be useful if you're writing a limerick. If you want to write a cinquain, check out "Ball and Glove" (page 9).

GLOSSARY

acrostic—a poem that uses the first letters of each line to spell out a word, name, or phrase relating to the poem's topic

alliteration—the use of two or more words that start with the same letter sound

ballad—a rhythmic poem that tells a story and is often sung

beat—a stressed word or syllable in a line of poetry

cinquain—a five-line poem that follows a 2-4-6-8-2 pattern of syllables

concrete poem—a poem that takes the shape of its subject

couplet—a pair of rhyming lines that usually have the same number of beats; couplets make their own point, create a separate image, or summarize the idea of a poem

dialogue—the words spoken between two or more characters (people or creatures); in writing, dialogue is set off with quotation marks

diamante—a seven-line poem that forms a diamond shape and follows this pattern: 1 noun, 2 adjectives, 3 verbs, 4 nouns, 3 verbs, 2 adjectives, 1 noun

free verse—a poem that follows no set rhythm or meter

haiku—a three-line poem that follows a 5-7-5 pattern of syllables

imagery—language that creates pictures in a reader's mind

limerick—a silly five-line poem in which the first two lines rhyme with the last, and the third and fourth lines rhyme with each other

lyric poem—a poem that expresses strong, personal feelings; sonnets, odes, and elegies are examples of lyric poetry

metaphor—a figure of speech that compares different things without using words such as "like" or "as"

meter—the pattern of beats in each line of a poem

narrative poem—a poem that tells a story

ode—a type of lyric poem, usually written in three stanzas with varying line lengths

personification—giving human characteristics, or traits, to something that isn't human

repetition—saying or doing something again and again

rhyme—word endings that sound the same

rhythm—a pattern of beats, like in music

simile—a figure of speech that compares different things by using the words "like" or "as"

stanza—a grouping of lines in poetry

stanza break—the blank line that separates stanzas in a poem

syllable—a unit of sound in a word

READ MORE

Fandel, Jennifer. *You Can Write Cool Poems*. You Can Write. North Mankato, Minn.: Capstone Press, 2012.

Prelutsky, Jack, poems selected by. *Read a Rhyme, Write a Rhyme*. New York: Alfred A. Knopf, 2005.

Salas, Laura Purdie. *Picture Yourself Writing Poetry: Using Photos to Inspire Writing*. See It, Write It. Mankato, Minn.: Capstone Press, 2012.

Silverstein, Shel. *Where the Sidewalk Ends: The Poems and Drawings of Shel Silverstein*. New York: HarperCollins, 2004.

Wilson, Karma. *Outside the Box*. New York: Margaret K. McElderry Books, 2013.

LOOK FOR ALL THE BOOKS IN THE SERIES:

PUCKS, CLUBS, AND BASEBALL GLOVES: READING AND WRITING SPORTS POEMS

THORNS, HORNS, AND CRESCENT MOONS: READING AND WRITING NATURE POEMS

TICKLES, PICKLES, AND FLOOFING PERSNICKLES: READING AND WRITING NONSENSE POEMS

TRUST, TRUTH, AND RIDICULOUS GOOFS: READING AND WRITING FRIENDSHIP POEMS

INTERNET SITES

FactHound offers a safe, fun way to find Internet sites related to this book. All of the sites on FactHound have been researched by our staff.

Here's all you do:
Visit www.facthound.com
Type in this code: 9781479521999

Super-cool stuff! Check out projects, games and lots more at **www.capstonekids.com**